Cooking For Abby: Corn-Free & GMO-Free Recipes

Also Contains Gluten-Free, Dairy-Free, Beef & Pork-Free, and Lower Histamine Recipes

by Diane Neuman

GW00455458

Table of Contents

Introduction

In 2011 our 16-year-old daughter had a muscle biopsy that showed a mitochondrial depletion. She at that time had developed chronic kidney disease, bladder issues, and GI issues.

We quickly found there are no cures or treatments for mitochondrial disease, or Mito. When Abby took medications for her kidneys or for her bladder, her symptoms quickly got worse instead of better. We then tried a cocktail of vitamins and supplements used for patients with Mito, and found that those made her symptoms worse as well.

Abby was sick as a baby and toddler. She had a lengthy list of food allergies (immunoglobulin E, or IgE, allergies) and poor muscle tone. Before age two, she had had a muscle biopsy and allergy testing. Her diagnosis at the time was an undefined congenital myopathy and food allergies. We were assured she would "outgrow" the muscle tone issues and the food allergies. We took it upon ourselves to change her diet to eliminate the foods that we knew caused her problems, and by the time she was six years or so, we found that she did indeed seem to be outgrowing her issues, as the doctors predicted. She blended well with the other children but struggled with allergies, asthma, frequent illness, and poor stamina. Overall, though, she was coping incredibly well and we felt her obstacles were no more than those faced by any other child.

At puberty she became ill again. Each year brought more and more health issues, to the point that school became impossible. Over the years we were assured again and again that she no longer had food allergies and it was impossible for her diet to be playing a role in her declining health.

We were panicked after that biopsy in 2011. Actually, we were in despair. What the specialists were telling us was that there was nothing we could do but treat the symptoms. The prognosis was grim.

We just could not accept that.

We felt that if her symptoms had improved when she was younger, then there had to be a way for them to improve again. As an infant, her allergies included soy, dairy, shellfish, tomato, and corn, among a few other things, so that is where we decided to start. Whether she had IgE allergies or not, we went on faith that food had been the key element in her healing as a toddler, and thus was a good place for us to start now.

We were so incredibly fortunate to meet many people who had discovered they too reacted to corn, soy, beets, wheat, and more. They taught us about the millions of places that GMO-corn is hidden in our food, about how medications and vitamins are filled with dairy, corn, and other items she seemed to be reacting to over the years. All of the members of the various health support groups have been fundamental in the positive progress Abby has made in the past three years.

Our first step was to remove gluten. Gluten can cause inflammation even in non-celiac people and many people struggle to digest it. Plus, a lot of the wheat in the US is treated heavily with Roundup, which some people believe lingers in the finished product, where it can have a negative effect on the body. Then we slowly eliminated the corn, which included all the corn derivatives. It can be found in the wax on fruit, in wax paper, in toilet paper, vitamins, medications, elemental and infant formulas, toothpaste, diapers, enriched foods, and many other products as well. Even citric acid is corn-derived. During the process of eliminating corn we quickly found out that if we wanted to feed her safely, we were going to have to learn to cook from scratch, like pioneers. While we were fortunate to grow up in a home where real, clean foods were readily available, we had, over the years, stocked our pantry with packaged and pre-made foods. We had become the all-American mac and cheese, pizza, take-out and eat-out family, and we knew that it had to stop immediately. When we stopped that behavior, we were rewarded with Abby's rapid improvement.

It has taken us three years to get to this point, where we feel reasonably confident that we have removed the worst of the corn, GMOs, high-histamine foods, chemicals (including insecticides, pesticides, and herbicides), and other random foods that her body has not done well with.

Her kidneys are doing remarkably well. We notice an increase in proteinuria when she is exposed to the smallest amount of corn, chemicals, or other GMOs. While she is not healed, she is stable, and while a few new issues have popped up, they have resolved on their own. She takes no medications, vitamins, or supplements at this time. We have simply been providing a safe and clean diet for her. We are very pleased to see her doing so well. Despite so many other patients with similar diagnosis having a more rapid progression of symptoms, Abby has mostly stabilized since removing all of the toxins from her diet. Her symptoms have slowed and some have resolved. Abby is on the right path now for better health. We will continue to improve the quality of her diet and environment and our greatest hope is that she can continue to show improvements.

This is a collection of recipes that we have created to avoid corn, GMOs, gluten, dairy, chemicals, and higher-histamine foods. Throughout our recipes we have tried to include some of the brand names that work for Abby. Please keep in mind that just because a brand or food is safe for Abby does not mean that it is safe for you. We suggest you do your own research on what is in your food to ensure your own safety. From a nutritionally balanced standpoint her diet is still lacking but we do the best we can for her based on what her body tolerates right now. Hopefully as she continues to improve and stay stable we can add more nutritionally dense foods to her diet.

A few exceptions: Lyle's golden syrup- while many of the recipes contain it, she doesn't consume it often. We have opted to allow it to be the one random food that might not be as clean as we would like. After all, she hasn't eaten anything we haven't cooked for her in three years, so it is an indulgence. Rice is another food that we know many view as an issue. Our goal has been to avoid rice that is enriched, since all enriched foods are contaminated with corn. I have found a few brands through our local international markets that she tolerates well and we will mention the brand names in the recipes. While we know there are concerns about arsenic and other contaminants that are found in rice, rice is a staple for Abby, and as long as she eats the brands that agree with her body, it has been fine. Lastly, I want to touch on the issue of sugar. Abby thrives on a simple carbohydrate diet. While we are well aware of the science, we have learned not to argue with Abby's body. As long as she continues to show improvements or maintain a better health status I have left well enough alone.

Bottom line: use the brands that are safe for you. This collection of recipes reflects the various creative problem solving we have done to try to recreate foods that appeal to a young adult. In this cookbook you can find simple food with a few funky ingredients. We have done our best to avoid GMOs and corn and the chemicals plaguing the Western diet that we feel contributed to Abby's once-declining health.

Thank you to all those who have mentored me and taught me how to take proper care of Abby. We owe you our gratitude. Without all of you, I know, without a doubt, that Abby's health would have continued to decline. She has you to thank for the improvements we are all so grateful to see in her each and every day.

The Basics

When I started cooking minus GMOs, corn, gluten, dairy, and nuts (among many other things), I quickly found that I was often missing key elements to our favorite recipes. I have come up with new elements to replace the ones we lost.

Coconut is one of the new cornerstones of Abby's diet. It is tasty and nutritious, and can take the place of dairy products; coconut yogurt and coconut sour cream have really allowed me to recreate many of our old favorites with a close to "normal" flavor for us. Another bonus to using coconut products is that it's much easier to find coconut that is safe and free of chemicals, pesticides, corn, and GMOs.

Chickpeas are another vital component to our diet. Abby is pretty limited on which meats she tolerates. She does well with chicken and eggs most of the time, but we still found her diet to be lacking in protein. Chickpeas have a terrific nutritional profile and are so versatile, especially when made into "nofu". Roasted chickpeas have also been essential as a replacement for the taste and texture of nuts and seeds.

While they aren't going to taste exactly the same, we quickly adjusted our taste buds and worked with the recipes to make the substitutions less noticeable.

In this segment of the book you will find recipes for these and other key components of Abby's diet. Recipes in the rest of the book will often refer back to these basics.

All-Purpose Gluten-Free Flour Blend

Ingredients:

*   3 ½ cups white rice flour
*   2 cups potato starch
*   1 cup teff flour (or other high-protein flour of your choice; other good options would be sorghum, ~~chick~~pea, or quinoa)   pea
*   1 ½ cups brown rice flour
*   1 cup tapioca starch

(If you opt to add guar gum, then add 4 teaspoons. As a general rule, you add ½ teaspoon guar gum per cup of gluten-free flour. Otherwise, omit guar gum from your all-purpose blend and add it only as needed for specific recipes.)

Directions:

Combine all ingredients in lidded container. Mix well and store in fridge.

You may need to whisk in the potato starch, as it can be lumpy.

Perfect Roasted Chickpeas

Perfect Roasted Chickpeas

Ingredients:

*   1 bag dried chickpeas
*   1 cup Trader Joe's grapeseed or Tropical Traditions coconut oil
*   salt to taste

Directions:

Soak your chickpeas overnight.

Cook your chickpeas, preferably in a pressure cooker, until they're so soft that some are in danger of bursting.

Drain cooked chickpeas well and let air dry for 30 minutes to 1 hour.

Line a full-sized cookie sheet with tinfoil and heat oven to 300°F.

Place cooked chickpeas on cookie sheet and evenly distribute them. It's okay if they're crowded; they shrink as they cook.

Pour ¾ cup of the oil over them.

Bake for 1 hour. After an hour, use a wooden spoon and stir them. Add the remaining ¼ cup of oil by drizzling it over any dry spots.

Bake for another hour, stirring every thirty minutes. At the 2-hour point, the oil should be foaming and sizzling.

Bake for another 30 minutes. Stir. The oil should be very foamy.

Bake for another 30 minutes. The foam should be settling down. Carefully remove a couple of chickpeas to a plate, let them cool for 1-2 minutes, and then try them. If they're crisp, they're ready to come out. If some are hard and some aren't, stir and put them back into the oven for another 15 minutes if necessary.

By the time they've baked for 3 hours and 30 minutes, they're surely done. Using a slotted spoon, scoop them out onto paper towels to drain, salting liberally every few spoonfuls.

Allow to cool and drain until room temperature, then transfer to an airtight container lined with paper towels.

They're ready to eat! You can season them, use them in recipes, or eat them plain.

Chickpea Nofu

Chickpea Nofu

Ingredients:

- 4 ½ cups water
- 1 ½ cups fine chickpea flour (grind your own or look for besan flour)
- dash of salt (pink Himalayan)
- 2 Tablespoons Trader Joe's grapeseed oil

Directions:

Mix the flour and water together until smooth in a container or bowl. Cover and let sit 12 hours or overnight.

If you use a clear container or bowl, you will see how it divides into a light colored liquid on top and an opaque thicker chickpea flour on the bottom.

Lightly oil a large pot (it will foam up during cooking) and your loaf pan.

Pour off the liquid part into your pot, saving the thicker bottom layer for later. Add salt, and bring to a boil.

Reduce heat to medium and stir continuously for 15 minutes. It is important to stir continuously to avoid lumps.

After 15 minutes pour the thicker reserved chickpea mixture from your container or bowl into the pot and stir for another 5 minutes. Be prepared, it thickens instantly and takes an intense effort to stir the remaining 5 minutes. It will be thick and almost gluey.

Pour the mixture into your loaf pan and refrigerate.

Coconut Nofu Cheese

When you have to be nut-free, soy-free, corn-free, dairy-free, and seed-free you realize that suddenly cheese is not an option.

This is a cheese substitute. It can be used as a replacement for cheese in anything from cheesecake to white sauce.

Add a bit of salt or fresh herbs to use as a spread for crackers or bread.

For use as a cream cheese replacement, add a little lemon juice or tamarind. Those ingredients will give it the tang associated with cream cheese.

The coconut yogurt can be strained on its own into a delicious cheese. This recipe adds chickpeas to give it more body so that it can be used as a topping on pizza or other dishes where cheese is melted.

Ingredients:

- 1 cup homemade coconut yogurt
- ⅓ cup very well-cooked chickpeas*

Canned chickpeas will be too firm. You need to cook the chickpeas until they are starting to fall apart. For best results, soak dried chickpeas and then cook them in a pressure cooker.

Directions:

For this recipe, you will need a yogurt cheese box and a piece of cotton muslin.

Combine the yogurt and chickpeas in a blender and purée until very smooth.

Line cheese strainer with a piece of wet/damp cotton muslin. Pour yogurt/cheese blend into the muslin.

Tie or twist the muslin shut. If your box has a lid, use it.

Leave at room temperature, squeezing every 1 to 2 hours to remove the whey.

After 8 hours of periodic squeezing, refrigerate overnight. In the morning, feel the muslin. If it is firm, you have removed enough whey. If it is still soft, allow it to come to room temperature, squeeze out more whey, and place back in the fridge.

Pull/scrape cheese off of the muslin and press it into a small, saran-lined container. Pack firmly and cover tightly and place back in fridge.

Refrigerate for a few hours before use.

Note: you can use many different methods to strain yogurt. You can also strain it by putting it inside a bag of cheesecloth and suspending it over a bowl to catch the whey.

Don't throw out the whey! You can use it for fermenting other things, or add it into another dish for added flavor and probiotics.

Lemon Curd

Lemon Curd

Ingredients:

* 5 fresh egg yolks
* 1 cup organic sugar (C&H)
* 2 organic lemons, zested and juiced*
* 5 Tablespoons coconut oil or palm shortening (Tropical Traditions)

Directions:

Add about an inch of water to a medium saucepan. Bring to a simmer on medium-high heat.

In a medium-sized glass bowl, combine egg yolks and sugar and whisk until smooth. This will take about 1 minute.

Measure out citrus juice and if needed, add enough cold water to your juice so that you have about ⅓ cup.

Add juice and zest to egg mixture and whisk smooth.

Once water reaches a simmer, reduce heat to medium and place bowl on top of saucepan. The bowl should be large enough to fit on top of the saucepan without touching the water.

Whisk constantly until thickened or until mixture is light yellow and coats the back of a spoon,

approximately 10 minutes. Remove promptly from heat.

Stir in coconut oil a spoonful at a time, allowing each addition to melt before adding the next.

Remove to a clean container and cover by laying a layer of plastic wrap directly on the surface of the curd.

Stir once an hour for the first few hours as the lemon curd chills. Coconut oil tends to float to the top, ruining your curd.

Keeps in refrigerator for up to 2 weeks.

Always gently scrub lemons with baking soda and warm water to remove any residual wax, which may have traces of corn, chemicals or other allergens in it.

Coconut Sour Cream

Ingredients:

- 1 cup of the coconut "cream" off of the top of a cold can of full-fat coconut milk (this will take approximately 2 cans of full-fat coconut milk; Arroy-D has a high fat content)
- 2 teaspoons of Bragg's apple cider vinegar

Directions:

Mix the cream of the coconut milk with the vinegar and refrigerate. You can add more or less vinegar depending on personal preferences.

A full-fat coconut milk is ideal. Coconut milks that are artificially thickened will not give you that hard cream at the top of the can. Experiment with different brands, or make your own coconut milk.

You can use the leftover coconut water for other recipes. It will keep in the fridge for up to a week.

Coconut Yogurt

In order to make your own allergen-free yogurt, you have to find a culture that is safe for you. Many popular cultures have traces of corn, soy, or dairy in them, which is enough to make some individuals react. Research cultures and be cautious. I discard all but a few Tablespoons of the first batch and use those couple Tablespoons to make a second generation batch to hopefully ensure the cleanest end result possible.

Ingredients:

- 3 cans coconut milk (no additives)
- 3 teaspoons sugar (organic C&H)
- 3 Tablespoons organic potato starch
- 3 heaping Tablespoons starter culture
- yogurt maker and thermometer

Preparation:

You can use freshly made coconut yogurt from either fresh coconut meat or dried coconut, but keep in mind that the less cream the coconut has, the less pleasing the final product will be. I skim a lot of the cream from a couple of batches of homemade coconut milk to make yogurt. The more cream the better the final texture. Arroy-D coconut milk is just coconut and water, so that is what this recipe will be using. (Thai Kitchens also has an organic full-fat coconut milk.)

The sugar is not optional. The bacteria you use to make yogurt need lactose to eat, which of course coconut milk lacks. You add in the sugar to give them the food they need. If you don't add sugar, your yogurt will not turn out as well.

You can use agar, gelatin, or tapioca starch instead of potato starch, but potato starch gives the most "normal" mouth feel.

For your starter, you can use So Delicious plain coconut yogurt. The first batch may contain trace allergens from the starter, but by the second generation batch the worst of that will be diluted out. Store bought yogurt is good for 4-6 batches. The greek yogurt dried culture starter from Cultures for Health creates a tangy coconut yogurt that we enjoy. For the first try or two I recommend a store bought coconut yogurt until you are comfortable.

The yogurt maker is optional. There are many ways to make yogurt. But you really need the thermometer so that you can put the culture into the coconut milk at the perfect moment. It needs to be warm, but cooled enough that it doesn't kill the bacteria. Temperature counts when making yogurt.

Make sure you use very clean containers and dishes. You don't want to culture the wrong bacteria.

Directions:

In a large pot, combine sugar and 2 cans of coconut milk. With the third can, add about ¾ of the can, reserving ¼ for later.

Slowly bring up to a slow boil, stirring occasionally.

While the coconut milk is warming, take the ¼ can of coconut milk you reserved and stir in the potato starch. Mix until very well-blended.

When the coconut milk is at a slow boil, grab a whisk and whisk in the potato starch mixture. It will thicken very quickly, so stir diligently. After a minute or so, the coconut milk should look like pudding. Remove from heat.

Allow the coconut milk mixture to cool to between 80-100°F. This will take awhile. Stir occasionally while it cools (with dairy you would place in an ice bath, but it is not needed when adding a thickener using coconut milk).

Once the temperature reaches 80-100°F, whisk in 3 heaping Tablespoons of starter culture. Whisk thoroughly.

Place mixture in yogurt maker, following yogurt maker's directions.

Leave it alone in the yogurt maker for 24 hours. Coconut yogurt takes extra culturing time. Whisk before putting it in the fridge. Allow to chill for at least 12 hours, 24 if possible.

After chilling, it's done. Save the last 3 or so Tablespoons of this batch to use to start your next.

Sweetened Condensed Coconut Milk

Sweetened condensed milk is an important ingredient in many recipes. If you cannot have dairy, this is a good alternative.

Ingredients:

- 2 cans coconut milk (or equivalent homemade; full-fat)
- 1 ½ cups sugar
- vanilla (homemade; *optional*)

Directions:

In saucepan, simmer slowly on medium-low heat, stirring occasionally, until reduced by approximately 50%. Add a touch of vanilla at this point if desired.

The key to this process is to maintain a very slow simmer to allow for evaporation.

Once finished, refrigerate. It will thicken as it chills, and may change in color to a very pale caramel color.

Nofu Butter

Abby cannot have nuts or seeds. This means no almond butter, no peanut butter, no tahini, no pumpkin seed butter, sunflower butter, or any other butter at all! With all these allergies, she ends up missing out on something as simple as a peanut butter sandwich, so we set out to make up for that loss.

Ingredients:

* 1 cup chickpea nofu
* 1 block or 1 cup coconut cream (this is different than the cream off of coconut milk; Tropical Traditions sells a coconut cream)
* ½ to 1 teaspoon salt (more or less to taste)
* 3 heaping Tablespoons organic dark brown sugar
* 3 Tablespoons grapeseed oil

Instructions:

Throw all ingredients into food processor. Blend repeatedly, scraping sides each time, until creamy and smooth.

You may add less or more brown sugar. More gives you more of a Jiffy taste, while less gives a more natural flavor.

Pack into jar and keep in fridge. Sometimes it can get too hard even with grapeseed oil; if this happens, set it on the counter an hour before it's needed.

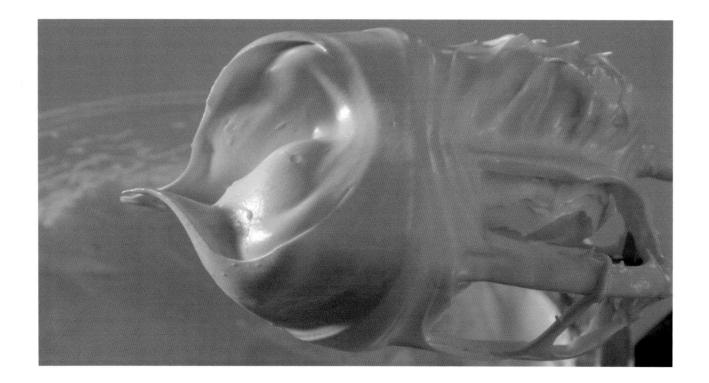

Marshmallow Frosting

Ingredients:

- 4 large egg whites
- 1 cup organic granulated sugar (C&H)
- 1 pinch salt (pink Himalayan)
- 1 teaspoon vanilla extract (homemade)

Directions:

Place all ingredients except vanilla into double boiler.

Whisk egg white mixture constantly over simmering water until the sugar dissolves and the mixture is hot- around 5 minutes.

Pour the mixture into stand mixer bowl or pour into large heat safe bowl and place on a hot pad and beat with electric mixer for 3 minutes. Add vanilla while beating. Mixture will be fluffy.

Use to top cupcakes or on a nofu butter sandwich. Will keep in the fridge for a week.

<u>Savory Recipes</u>

You will find in this section that our recipes also exclude beef, pork, tomatoes, and a few other common vegetables. Abby reacts to many foods, not just GMOs, and through our journey to find safer foods for her we have had to learn to enjoy a number of foods that we either never tried before or that simply were not part of our weekly grocery shopping.

We try to include as much nutrition as we can within Abby's limited diet, and part of that involves being open to trying new foods.

But you will also find in this section that it is possible to make delicious food from unfamiliar ingredients. There are some old favorites like biscuits and gravy, spaghetti, and even corn-free cornbread that can be recreated on Abby's diet.

If you keep an open mind, I'm sure that you'll find yourself enjoying these recipes too.

Softest Ever Gluten-Free Tortillas

You will need an electric tortilla maker for this recipe.*

Ingredients:

- 2 ½ cups all-purpose gluten-free flour
- 2 teaspoons guar gum (NOW brand)
- 1 teaspoon organic granulated sugar (Domino's or C&H)
- ½ cup tapioca starch
- 1 teaspoon salt
- 2 ½ teaspoons baking powder (homemade)
- 4 Tablespoons coconut oil (Tropical Traditions)
- 1 ¾ – 2 cups warm water (I keep extra on hand, wetter is better with this recipe)

Directions:

Preheat tortilla press on highest heat setting with lid open.

In a large mixing bowl, combine dry ingredients with coconut oil until it is slightly crumbly.

Add in warm water until the dough reaches a wet and sticky consistency and look, almost like a stretchy brownie batter. This may require you to add more water than is called for in the ingredient list. When in doubt, let it sit for 5 minutes after adding 1 ¾ cups, then assess whether it needs more water or not. You want to be able to place a soft blob on the press that just barely holds its shape. A wetter batter is better than a drier one.

Once the tortilla press is heated all the way, lightly grease it if desired. Place a generous Tablespoon of batter (slightly less than ¼ cup) on the tortilla press. Beginners are advised to place the batter a tiny touch off-center, towards the hinge. Close the press and push down hard on the handle one at a time. You will hear a squealing sound as steam escapes around the edges. You want the sound of steam escaping, but you need to avoid pressing so hard that you hear it pop. The pop means the tortilla will be ripped.

Immediately lift the pressing handle and raise the lid a bit to release steam pressure, then gently close the lid and allow the tortilla to cook for approximately 60 seconds. Then open the press, flip the tortilla, and close the lid to cook for another 10-20 seconds. The tortilla is now done!

You can stack them right on top of each other on a plate, but if you later pull them apart too fast they may stick together and tear. They tend to be slightly crisp when they come out, but when they're stacked on top of each other they relax and become soft and elastic.

To reheat, you can steam them in a rice cooker. They will be almost as good as fresh if you steam them for a couple of minutes. You can reheat tortillas that are up to a week old this way, with good results. You can also heat stale tortillas briefly in the microwave to soften them.

Getting used to using an electric tortilla press will take some time and practice, especially when dealing with gluten-free. Every recipe will require a slightly different method. Once you get used to using the tortilla press, you'll find that making tortillas is much less difficult and messy.

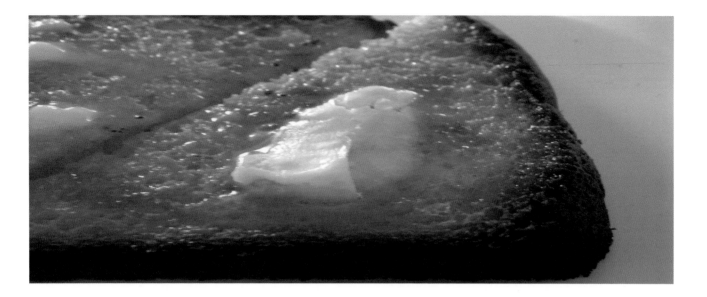

Faux Butter Spread

Ingredients:

- ½ cup grapeseed oil
- ½ cup coconut oil (Tropical Traditions)
- ½ teaspoon salt (or more to taste)
- ¼ teaspoon turmeric (for color)
- ½ teaspoon Lyle's golden syrup or granulated sugar for sweet butter (*optional*)

Directions:

Place oil, coconut oil, salt, and turmeric into a saucepan. Add granulated sugar if desired. Warm on low temperature until coconut oil is melted and salt has mostly dissolved.

Pour into stand mixture or hand mixture bowl and place in fridge for approximately 30 minutes. You don't want to chill it completely or it will be too hard to whip; aim for about half solidified.

Whip with mixer until light and well-blended. This only takes a minute or so.

For a sweeter, more buttery spread add barely ½ teaspoon of Lyle's golden syrup. This syrup has a slight buttery flavor, and the slight sweetness makes it so that the spread isn't just fat flavored. I find as well that the bit of syrup keeps the spread softer.

Buckwheat Stuffed Peppers

Buckwheat Stuffed Peppers

[handwritten: stuffing]

Ingredients:

- 1 cup toasted buckwheat groats (toast raw buckwheat in pan until they start bursting; they'll be a little puffy and show some white)
- 3 cups homemade chicken broth
- 1 diced organic onion
- ½ cup mushrooms (any kind)
- ½ cup frozen or fresh organic peas
- 1 cup chopped fresh baby bok choy
- ½ teaspoon Simply Organic dried thyme
- 2 eggs *[handwritten: yolks only]*
- 2 Tablespoons homemade coconut yogurt
- salt and pepper to taste
- quail (or chicken) eggs to serve on top of stuffed pepper (*optional*)

Directions:

Preheat oven to 350°F.

Sauté onion and mushrooms until soft.

In saucepan, combine buckwheat, chicken broth, mushrooms, onions, and thyme. Bring to boil and then reduce heat to low for approximately 15 minutes until all the chicken broth is absorbed. Remove from heat. Add peas and salt and pepper to taste. Allow to cool while you prepare red peppers.

Cut the tops off your peppers and remove ribs and seeds. Beat together eggs and coconut yogurt.

After peppers are prepared and buckwheat is cooled, mix beaten egg/yogurt mixture and baby bok choy into buckwheat. Fill peppers with resultant mixture and cover them.

Bake for approximately 30-40 minutes and serve.

To add richness, fry an egg (pictured: quail) and slide on top of finished stuffed pepper (*optional*).

Rice Pot Chicken & Rice

Rice Pot Chicken & Rice

Ingredients:

(chicken rice)

- 2 cups non-enriched rice (and the appropriate amount of water or chicken broth)
- 1 red pepper
- 1 Tablespoon finely grated fresh ginger
- 1 teaspoon tumeric (fresh is best, powdered is fine)
- 1 finely sliced chicken breast
- salt and pepper to taste

(baby bok choy)

- a few handfuls fresh baby bok choy (ends cut off, cleaned well)
- 1-2 cloves of finely minced fresh or roasted garlic
- coconut oil

Directions:

(chicken rice)

Sauté red pepper and ginger to make sure they're tender. It's important that the chicken is sliced very thinly; otherwise you can't be sure it will cook completely.

Add all ingredients to rice pot, stir, and cook on the rice function.

(baby bok choy)

Sauté the garlic on the stovetop in the coconut oil.

Add the baby bok choy. Cover with the lid and cook for only a few minutes, shaking the pot occasionally to make sure all the bok choy is cooked. When the bok choy begins to wilt, it's done.

Serve rice and bok choy together.

Irish Soda Bread

Ingredients:

- 4 cups gluten-free flour blend
- 2 Tablespoons sugar (coconut or organic cane sugar)
- 2 teaspoons baking soda
- 4 teaspoons baking powder (homemade)
- 1 teaspoon guar gum (NOW brand)
- 1 ½ Tablespoons psyllium husk powder (NOW brand)
- 1 teaspoon salt (pink Himalayan or sea salt)
- 2 eggs
- 2 Tablespoons grapeseed oil
- 2 cups milk of choice (suggested: ¾ cup coconut yogurt mixed with 1 ¼ cups water)
- 1 Tablespoon Bragg's apple cider vinegar

Irish Soda Bread

Directions:

Preheat oven to 375°F. Lightly grease loaf pan.

Mix all dry ingredients in a bowl.

Add egg, milk, and oil, and mix to form a soft, sticky dough. It should be not quite thick enough to be a dough, but not soft enough to be a batter.

Add vinegar last and quickly mix it in.

Place dough in greased pan. Wet hands with water and smooth out top so it's higher in the middle and looks more loaf-like.

Use a wet knife and cut a deep cross in the top. Dust with gluten-free flour.

Allow to sit on the counter for about 10 minutes. This lets the baking soda and vinegar provide a bit of lift before it hits the heat of the oven.

Bake for 35-40 minutes.

Allow to cool, then slice and store in an airtight container.

Gluten-Free Dairy-Free Corn-Free Cornbread

Gluten-Free Dairy-Free Corn-Free Cornbread

This faux cornbread recipe uses chickpea flour, which can taste a little bean-like when raw to some taste buds, but even the most skeptical members of my family can attest that it worked quite well in this recipe. It tastes very much like regular cornbread.

Ingredients:

* 1 cup gluten-free all-purpose flour
* ½ cup chickpea flour
* ½ cup millet flour (coarsely grind millet seed in the blender to fake the cornmeal texture)
* 3 Tablespoons of organic cane sugar (C&H)
* 2 ½ teaspoons baking powder (homemade)
* ¾ teaspoon salt (pink Himalayan)
* 3 Tablespoons grapeseed oil or melted coconut oil (Tropical Traditions)
* 2-3 beaten eggs (use 2 for a more crumbly texture, and 3 for a more cake-like texture)
* 1-3 Tablespoons local honey, to taste
* 1 cup rice milk or coconut milk (homemade)

Directions:

Preheat the oven to 400°F. Grease 8x8 pan with coconut or grapeseed oil.

Mix the dry ingredients (flours, millet, sugar, baking powder, and salt) together in a medium-sized bowl and set aside.

In a small bowl, combine the eggs, rice or coconut milk, and ¼ cup oil.

Add wet ingredients to the flour mixture and stir until dry ingredients are just moistened.

Pour batter into baking pan and bake for 20-25 minutes or until a wooden toothpick comes out clean. Serve warm.

Chicken Breakfast Sausage Patties

Chicken Breakfast Sausage Patties

These patties work terrifically with an egg and homemade gluten-free english muffins, or on Thai-inspired waffles... or on their own! You will need ground chicken breast for this recipe; I recommend grinding your own. Buying local chicken from your local farmer allows you to make sure it was not fed GMOs or rinsed in citric acid when butchering.

Ingredients:

- 1 ½ pounds ground chicken breast ~grind up
- ¼ cup finely ground gluten-free bread crumbs (dry leftover gluten-free bread and grind it in a food processor)
- 1 teaspoon salt (to taste)
- 1 ½ teaspoons freshly ground black pepper
- 2 teaspoons ground sage leaves
- 2 teaspoons ground thyme leaves
- 1 teaspoon fresh rosemary (dried acceptable)
- 1 Tablespoon maple syrup (grade B or stronger)
- ½ teaspoon fresh grated nutmeg
- ½ teaspoon cayenne pepper (to taste)
- ½ teaspoon red pepper flakes
- grapeseed oil or coconut oil (Tropical Traditions)

Directions:

Combine ingredients, except for the grapeseed oil, and chill for 1 hour. Form into 1-inch rounds. Refrigerate and use within 1 day or freeze for up to 3 months.

To prepare, sauté patties over medium-low heat in a non-stick pan with a bit of grapeseed oil. Adding grapeseed or coconut oil to fry would be unnecessary with normal sausage, but chicken breast is so lean that it will stick if you don't add oil.

Sauté until brown and cooked through. This will take approximately 10-15 minutes, depending on the thickness of your sausage patties.

Spicy Biscuits and Chicken Gravy

Ingredients:

* biscuits or bread
* 2-3 cooked chicken sausage patties
* crushed red pepper flakes
* cayenne powder
* salt
* coconut oil (Tropical Traditions)
* rice milk and coconut milk (rice milk is too watery and coconut milk on its own can have a strong coconut flavor, but an equal amount of both is a nice blend)
* ¼ cup all-purpose gluten-free flour blend

Directions:
Heat sausage in saucepan along with spices. Brown for a few minutes.

Mix ¼ cup gluten-free flour with 1 cup of coconut milk. Blend with a whisk until there are no lumps. Turn stovetop heat up to medium-high and pour the milk/flour mixture into the sausage. Keep stirring briskly with the whisk to avoid lumps.

Keep a cup of rice milk ready, because the gravy will thicken as it is being whisked and you want to keep it thick but still pourable.

ALTERNATE METHOD: Add flour directly to sausage, and mix until it's all coating the sausage and is damp with oil. Then add milk and whisk as normal. This can be an easier method for people who end up with lumps no matter how much they whisk. It may not work if your sausage is very lean.

Once it comes to a boil your flour will have cooked and it is ready to serve.

Uncle Mike's Potato Pancakes

Ingredients:

- 2 cups mashed organic potatoes (I use coconut yogurt to make mashed potatoes)
- 2 eggs ~ yolks only
- 2 heaping Tablespoons gluten-free flour
- 2 Tablespoons very finely minced (or grated) yellow onion

Directions:

Start warming a frying pan on medium heat. Mix ingredients thoroughly in single bowl.

In heated pan, add a Tablespoon of coconut oil. Keep heat on medium; it's best to cook this slowly, to ensure they cook all the way through.

Scoop a portion of your potato mixture into the pan. Spread it out with the back of your spoon so that it's smooth and even. Flip when bottom is golden. These take a little longer than a pancake to cook, be patient.

Top with granulated sugar, pear or apple sauce, and coconut sour cream.

Buckwheat Gluten-Free Loaf

Buckwheat makes a dense loaf. It will also add much needed nutrition and flavor. In the past I have added ground caraway and whole caraway seed, dill weed, and substituted ¼ cup pickle juice for the water. Those modifications will result in something similar to rye bread. As it is below, it's just a nice wholesome bread that we use to replace whole wheat bread in our diet.

- 1 ½ cups coconut milk (homemade)
- ¾ cup water
- 3 eggs *yolks only*
- 1 Tablespoon Bragg's apple cider vinegar
- 2 Tablespoons Trader Joe's grapeseed oil
- 1 Tablespoon organic C&H cane sugar
- 2 Tablespoons organic Plantation blackstrap molasses
- 3 cups all-purpose gluten-free flour (homemade)
- 1 cup buckwheat flour
- 1 teaspoon salt (pink Himalayan)
- 1 Tablespoon NOW brand guar gum
- 1 Tablespoon active dry yeast (for corn-free, use Red Star active, not rapid)

Place in order given by your bread machine. I used the basic function with dark crust option in the Zojirushi.

NOTE: I have found the amount of liquid needed can vary depending on the buckwheat flour. It will be a thicker than normal batter/dough but it still should move freely in the bread maker. Adjustment to liquid (water) may be needed.

Teff Bread Machine Loaf

Ingredients:

- 1 ½ cups coconut milk (homemade)
- 3 eggs
- 1 Tablespoon Bragg's apple cider vinegar
- 2 Tablespoons grapeseed oil
- 2 Tablespoons local honey
- 3 cups all purpose gluten-free flour (homemade)
- 1 cup Ivory Teff Company teff flour
- 1 teaspoon salt (pink Himalayan)
- 1 Tablespoon NOW brand guar gum
- 1 Tablespoon active dry yeast (active not rapid)

Directions:

Place ingredients in the pan of the bread machine in the order recommended by the manufacturer. 5 minutes into the cycle, check the consistency of the dough. Add additional flour or liquid if necessary.

When bread is finished, let cool for 10 to 15 minutes before removing from pan.

Halloween Soup

Ingredients:

- 4 cups chicken broth (homemade)
- 1 chicken breast
- 3 carrots, peeled and sliced
- 1 small sweet onion, diced
- basil
- parsley
- thyme
- salt
- King Soba brand black rice noodles

Directions:

In large saucepan, add broth and chicken breast. Bring to a boil and then simmer for 30 minutes or until chicken breast is cooked. Add carrots, onion, and seasoning. Simmer/low boil for another 30 minutes. Remove chicken breast, dice it and put the diced chicken back into pot. Add rice noodles and cook for 10 minutes more.

Use fresh, organic herbs when possible.

The black noodles tend to bleed some of their color into the broth, giving the broth a dark coloration. In combination with the orange carrots, it looks like Halloween!

This freezes fairly well, though the rice noodles tend to break down with freezing. We usually remove the noodles before freezing the soup in single portion sized containers.

nofu ramen soup with pea greens, mushrooms, celery, carrot, and green onion

Nofu Ramen Soup

Ingredients:

- 3 cups chicken or beef broth (homemade)
- ½ cup pressed and diced nofu (homemade)
- 3 Tablespoons Coconut Secret Coconut Aminos (similar to soy sauce)
- ¼ cup thinly peeled organic celery
- ¼ cup thinly peeled organic carrot
- 2 Tablespoons sliced organic green onions
- ½ cup pea leaves
- 1 teaspoon fresh grated ginger
- chili flakes or Thai peppers
- mushrooms

Directions:

Boil your noodles. Rinse with cold water and set aside.

Bring your broth to a boil and add ginger, chili flakes, coconut aminos, and whatever other seasonings you like.

Add the nofu to the boiling broth and allow to cook for 5 minutes.

Place your noodles and veggies in your bowl and pour the broth over the top. Serve.

Socca Bread

Socca Bread

Ingredients:

- 1 cup chickpea (besan) flour
- 1 cup water
- 1 Tablespoon coconut or grapeseed oil
- seasoning of your choice (I use about 1 Tablespoon of fresh rosemary)
- 1 diced onion

Directions:

Combine water and chickpea flour, mix until smooth.

You can keep the bean flour mixture in the fridge. I often make the batter the night before. I find that if I let the batter rest for at least a couple hours before baking, the socca has the best texture.

Preheat oven to 425°F.

Your choice of pan will depend on how you want your socca to turn out. A smaller pan will make a thicker and softer socca, and a bigger pan will make thinner and chewier socca. Thin, chewy socca would make a great pizza crust.

Add fresh rosemary and diced onion to batter.

Add oil to pan and heat the pan until very hot (5-10 minutes). Pour your batter into the pan and bake for 35-40 minutes.

Serve hot.

Tomato-Free Red Sauce (Red Pepper Sauce)

Tomato-Free Red Sauce (Red Pepper Sauce)

This spaghetti sauce uses roasted red peppers instead of tomatoes. Along with being delicious on pasta, this sauce is great for pizza, meatloaf, and sloppy joes. Cutting out tomatoes doesn't have to mean cutting out these foods!

Ingredients:

- 4 red peppers
- 2 sweet yellow onions
- 3 cloves of garlic
- Italian seasoning
- parsley
- 1 teaspoon sugar (*optional*)
- grapeseed oil (for heating vegetables)

Directions:

Heat oven to 400°F.

Place the peppers on a baking tray and place in oven for about 45 minutes until their skin is blackened. After 20 minutes, flip and do other side.

Remove them from the oven and immediately put them into a plastic bag and seal. This makes them sweat, which makes the skin easier to remove.

When cool enough to handle, peel off the skins with your fingers. Slice the peppers open, pick out and discard the seeds and membranes, then roughly chop the remaining flesh.

Chop your onions and garlic and sauté together with the chopped roasted peppers in grapeseed oil.

Add seasonings and simmer for 20 minutes.

Once cool, place sautéed peppers, onions, garlic, and seasonings into a blender and purée them.

Use immediately or refrigerate for later use. Keeps in fridge for up to a week and it also freezes well.

If the peppers are not very sweet, you may add a little bit of sugar to the purée. Keeping the sauce in the fridge overnight deepens the flavors.

Tomato-Free Spinach-Free Italian Meatball Soup

Tomato-Free Spinach-Free Italian Meatball Soup

This recipe uses a chicken bone broth, and roasted red pepper sauce which is already seasoned with Italian-based herbs. I usually have frozen broth, roasted red pepper sauce, and chicken meatballs in the freezer so this is very quick to put together.

Ingredients:

- 4 cups homemade chicken broth
- 1 ½ cups roasted red pepper sauce
- 12 chicken meatballs (or more or less, to your preference)
- ½ teaspoon oregano
- handful of fresh chopped basil
- season and salt to taste

Directions:

Combine broth, red pepper sauce, and basil.

Bring to boil and add pre-cooked chicken meatballs. I make chicken meatballs and keep them frozen and ready to use.

Season to your liking and serve.

Corned Chicken Hash

True corned beef is made by putting a brisket in a brine for 10 days. As there is a greater risk of chicken carrying dangerous bacteria, this is not a good idea. We came up with this quick imitation version for people who cannot eat beef.

Corned Chicken Hash

Ingredients:

- 1 diced, cooked organic chicken breast
- 1 diced and peeled organic potato (around same amount as chicken pieces)
- 1 finely diced organic onion
- 1 finely diced or organic shredded carrot
- 1 Tablespoon coconut oil

(pickling spices)

- 1 bay leaf
- 2 teaspoons organic brown sugar or local honey
- 2 teaspoons apple cider vinegar
- ½ cup water
- parsley flakes

(and equal amounts of)

- allspice
- ground mustard
- red pepper flakes
- ground cloves
- coarse ground black peppercorns
- ground cardamom
- ground ginger

Directions:

Combine all pickling ingredients to Ziploc bag.

Add diced chicken to pickling liquid. Seal bag and make sure that all pieces are being bathed in fluid.

Place bag in bowl and marinate for at least 1 hour and ideally overnight in the fridge.

Once well-marinated, drain the marinade from the chicken and add the chicken, potato, onion, and carrot to a skillet with melted coconut oil in it.

Cover and cook on medium-low until potatoes and carrots are tender (approximately 30 minutes). You can uncover and turn up the heat for the last 10 minutes to get some browning on the hash. Don't mix too much after the cooking process is well underway, otherwise you will turn your hash into mash.
If your hash begins to look dry at any point in the cooking, add a Tablespoon or so of chicken broth or a teaspoon of coconut oil.

Serve with fried eggs.

Dairy-Free, Soy-Free, Corn-Free, Vegan Potato Soup

Ingredients:

(for the "bacon")
- chickpea nofu
- coconut aminos
- maple syrup (know your source, even 100% "real" can be tainted with de-foamers)
- apple cider vinegar
- organic dark brown sugar
- salt (pink Himalayan)

(for the soup)
- 3 scrubbed, peeled, and diced organic potatoes
- 1 diced organic yellow onion
- 2 grated organic carrots
- 1 Tablespoon dried or fresh parsley
- salt and pepper to taste
- 1-2 cups plain coconut yogurt (add more for richer soup)
- 1 cup cold plain rice milk
- 1 Tablespoon potato starch (mixed into milk)

Dairy-Free, Soy-Free, Corn-Free, Vegan Potato Soup

Directions:

(for "bacon")

First, create a marinade to soak the chickpea nofu in. Combine equal amounts of everything except the vinegar and salt; use just a dash of vinegar and a shake of salt.

Cut nofu as thin as possible without breaking it. Press slices between paper towels for about an hour; cover with something heavy, like a book or cans of food.

Then in a dry non-stick pan (with no oil in it) turn the burner on low and carefully add slices of nofu. Cook very slowly, uncovered, and flip frequently. Until it begins to dry it will be sticky; flip carefully in the beginning.

Cook slowly for 30-40 minutes on the lowest possible setting, flipping every 5-10 minutes and gently pressing each slice.

Once it seems dry (should not be darker than golden brown, usually cracks a little), remove from heat and put the pieces in the marinade. Cover nofu in marinade and refrigerate overnight. You can soak them for even 2 days without the slices getting mushy. If they get mushy, you didn't get them dry enough.

After marinating, grill the nofu hard either on the stovetop or grill. The sugars in the marinade will caramelize and brown up nicely. When it is nice and brown, remove from heat. Dice and salt heavily. Then fry in coconut oil until very crisp.

(the soup)

Throw onions, potatoes, carrots, and parsley into pot, with a couple of cups of water to cover them. You could use chicken stock instead of water here for a non-vegan version or instead of water a vegetable stock. It takes around 15-30 minutes of boiling until they are soft.

Mix in yogurt, salt, and pepper to your broth and veggies.

Slowly add in rice milk about ¼ cup at a time to make sure it doesn't thicken too much.

At this point you are done. Top with chickpea bacon. You could also add green onion or peas for extra color.

Abby Style Tzatziki Sauce

Ingredients:

- 2 cups homemade plain coconut yogurt
- 1 organic cucumber, unpeeled and seeded
- 1 Tablespoon plus ½ teaspoon salt
- ½ cup homemade coconut sour cream
- 1 Tablespoon Bragg's apple cider vinegar
- 2 Tablespoons freshly squeezed organic lemon juice (1 lemon)
- 1 Tablespoon grapeseed oil
- 1 ½ teaspoons fresh minced garlic
- 1 ½ teaspoons minced fresh dill (dried works fine)
- pinch freshly ground black pepper

Directions:

Place the coconut yogurt in a cheesecloth or paper towel-lined sieve and set it over a bowl. Grate the cucumber and toss it with 1 Tablespoon of salt; place it in another sieve, and set it over another bowl. Place both bowls in the refrigerator for 3 to 4 hours so the coconut yogurt and cucumber can drain.

Transfer the thickened coconut yogurt to a bowl. Squeeze as much liquid from the cucumber as you can and add the cucumber to the coconut yogurt. Mix in the coconut sour cream, vinegar, lemon juice, olive oil, garlic, dill, ½ teaspoon salt, and pepper.

Refrigerate for a few hours for the flavors to blend. Serve chilled.

Chicken Jerky

Ingredients:

- partially frozen organic/clean chicken breast (fat trimmed)
- 1 cup coconut aminos
- ¼ cup coconut vinegar
- 1 Tablespoon organic lemon juice
- pink Himalayan salt
- 2 teaspoons organic sugar
- ginger powder
- garlic powder

Directions:

Add all marinade ingredients to Ziploc bag (you may alter amounts of ingredients to suit your tastes).

Cut chicken breast into extremely thin strips, cutting against the grain.

Place strips into bag, place bag into bowl, and marinate in fridge overnight.

After marinating, place in dehydrator and follow manufacturer's directions.

With poultry jerky, it is essential that after pulling the jerky from the dehydrator, you place the jerky in the oven at 200°F (or lower) for 10-15 minutes. The dehydrator does not get hot enough to kill potential bacteria. Watch the jerky carefully once in the oven because of the sugars in the marinade; you don't want it to burn.

Myacoba Bean Stew with Pea Leaves and Paprika Chicken

Myacoba Bean Stew with Pea Leaves and Paprika Chicken

Ingredients:
- ½ cup grapeseed oil
- 2 large carrots, chopped
- 2 large shallots or 1 yellow onion, chopped
- 2 ½ cups white beans, soaked overnight
- 8 cups homemade chicken broth
- 4 bay leaves
- 1 teaspoon dried thyme
- salt and pepper to taste
- 1 chicken breast, cooked and shredded
- 1 cup pea greens
- 2 teaspoons smoked paprika
- 1-2 teaspoons organic C&H sugar

Directions:

Sauté the shallots and carrots in a large pot until the shallots are tender.

Add chicken broth, beans, bay leaves, and thyme.

Cover and cook for 1 ½ to 2 hours until the beans are extremely tender but still holding their shape.

Pull about half the cooked beans out and reserve. Pour the rest of the soup and beans into the blender and purée until smooth. Salt to taste and keep warm.

Next, add oil to a frying pan and then add about half the chicken breast, reserving half of the breast plain.

Sprinkle with paprika, sugar, and salt. Cook until sugar is melted and is aromatic.

In a small saucepan boil a cup of water and quickly blanch the pea leaves, then drain.

To serve, pour some purée into a bowl, then add the reserved beans and plain chicken breast. Top with wilted pea leaves and seasoned chicken before serving.

Sweet Recipes

One of the biggest challenges we faced going GMO-free was in making desserts. Learning to bake gluten-free would have been a challenge unto itself, but when we had to cut out dairy, soy, and nuts (among other things) all at the same time, it felt impossible. Little by little, we tried different combinations, and we came up with what we feel are some creative solutions to the challenges posed by Abby-safe baking.

One thing that we don't worry about in baking is sugar content. High-fat foods can sometimes upset Abby's stomach, but we don't worry as much about those either. At the end of the day, no one *needs* dessert, but who wants to? We certainly don't. I just try to increase nutrition wherever I can; adding an extra egg to a recipe or using a high-protein flour blend can make a tasty treat a little less guilty.

Abby's Favorite Gluten-Free Yellow Cake

Abby's Favorite Gluten-Free Yellow Cake

Ingredients:

(cake)
- 2 ¼ cups all-purpose gluten-free flour
- 1 teaspoon salt
- 1 teaspoon baking soda
- 3 teaspoons baking powder
- 1 teaspoon guar gum
- 4 eggs
- 1 ½ cups organic C&H cane sugar
- ⅔ cup homemade coconut yogurt
- 1 Tablespoon grapeseed oil
- 1 cup homemade rice milk
- 2 teaspoons vanilla extract (homemade)

(frosting)
- carob powder (check ingredients and source carefully)
- corn-free powdered sugar
- Tropical Traditions palm shortening
- homemade rice milk
- vanilla extract (homemade)

Directions:

Preheat oven to 350°F degrees.

Grease and flour two 8 or 9 inch round cake pans, or line cupcake tins.

Mix the flour, salt, baking soda, baking powder, and guar gum together and set aside.

Mix the eggs, sugar, grapeseed oil and coconut yogurt until fluffy.

Combine wet and dry ingredients and mix well. You will get a thin batter. Pour batter into prepared pans.

Bake for 22-25 minutes. For cupcakes, bake 15-18 minutes. Cakes are done when they spring back when lightly touched or when a toothpick inserted near the center comes out clean.

Beat together frosting ingredients with mixer to get carob frosting. Frost cake liberally.

Animal Crackers

Ingredients:

* 1 ½ cups all-purpose gluten-free flour
* ¾ teaspoon NOW brand guar gum
* ½ teaspoon baking powder (homemade)
* ⅛ teaspoon baking soda
* 2 Tablespoons homemade coconut yogurt
* ¼ teaspoon salt
* ¼ cup organic granulated sugar (Domino's or C&H)
* ¼ cup packed light brown sugar (Domino's or homemade)
* 4 Tablespoons Tropical Traditions palm shortening at room temperature
* 1 extra-large egg
* 1 teaspoon vanilla extract (homemade)

Directions:

Preheat oven to 350°F.

Mix all the dry ingredients, and then add in everything else. You may have to work this by hand to get it to stick together into a dough.

Flour the counter and roll out dough to a thickness of about ½ inch. Cut out cookies with animal cookie cutters.

You don't have to worry about crowding the cookie sheet; these puff up, but don't spread.

Place cookie sheet (with the raw cookies on it) into freezer for at least 15 minutes. This step is important. These cookie cutters are so small that even a little bit of spread will distort them.

Remove from freezer and bake for 8-9 minutes, until cookies are showing a bit of golden around edges. Allow to cool and keep them in an airtight container.

No Oats Oatmeal Cookies

Ingredients:
- 2 ½ cups toasted glutinous rice flakes (pinipig or thin poha)
- ½ cup toasted coconut flakes (Tropical Traditions)
- 1 ¾ cups all-purpose gluten-free flour
- ½ teaspoon salt
- 1 teaspoon baking soda
- 1 teaspoon allspice (or cinnamon)
- ½ teaspoon cloves
- ¼ cup organic white sugar (Domino's or C&H)
- 1 cup brown sugar (Domino's or homemade)
- 1 cup palm shortening (Tropical Traditions)
- 2 large eggs
- 1 teaspoon vanilla extract (homemade)
- 1 ½ cups chopped home dried cherries and chopped Made in Nature brand black mission figs (or raisins)

Directions:

Preheat oven to 350°F. Line a cookie sheet with parchment paper.

Cream shortening and sugars together. Add eggs and vanilla. Stir in flour, salt, spices, and baking soda.

Stir in rice flakes and raisins last.

Place one cookie onto the cookie sheet and bake 8-10 minutes as a trial. If it flattens too much, add ¼ cup more flour.

Place cookies a couple of inches apart on cookie sheet. Bake 8-10 minutes or until lightly browned. Allow to cool before removing from tray.

Microwave Chickpea Brittle

Ingredients:

- 1 cup white sugar (Domino's organic cane sugar)
- ½ cup Lyle's golden syrup
- 1 cup salted roasted chickpeas
- 1 teaspoon palm shortening (Tropical Traditions)
- 1 teaspoon vanilla extract (homemade)
- 1 teaspoon baking soda

Directions:

Generously grease a cookie sheet.

Combine sugar and Lyle's golden syrup in a 2-quart glass bowl and microwave on high for 4 minutes.

Stir in roasted chickpeas and microwave on high 3 ½ minutes.

Stir in palm shortening and vanilla and microwave for 1 ½ minutes.

Stir in baking soda until light and foamy.

Pour onto cookie sheet and spread thin.

Cool completely, then break into pieces and store in airtight container.

Fried Rosette Cookies

Fried Rosette Cookies

Ingredients:

- 1 cup all-purpose gluten-free flour
- 1 cup coconut milk or rice milk
- ½ teaspoon salt
- 3 teaspoons sugar
- 1 egg
- ½ teaspoon vanilla extract
- oil or shortening for frying
- corn-free powdered sugar for sprinkling
- rosette maker

Directions:

Mix all ingredients in blender until very smooth.

Pour mixture into flat-bottomed bowl.

Heat rosette iron for 2 minutes in oil heated to 375°F.

Drain excess oil from iron by quickly blotting iron on paper towels.

Dip in batter to ¼ inch from the top of iron, being careful not to go over the top. If you go over the top, the cookie will not release properly. Then dip iron immediately into the hot oil.

Fry rosette until golden, about 30 seconds. Lift out; tip upside down to drain. With fork, push rosette off iron onto a rack placed over paper towels.

Reheat iron for 1 minute. Repeat process until all batter is gone.

Sprinkle finished rosettes with corn-free powdered sugar.

Coconut Cream Pie

Ingredients:

(gluten-free pie crust)
- 1 ¼ cups gluten-free all-purpose flour
- 1 Tablespoon sugar (C&H or Domino's organic cane sugar)
- ½ teaspoon guar gum (NOW brand)
- ½ teaspoon salt (pink Himalayan)
- 6 Tablespoons cold palm shortening (Tropical Traditions)
- 1 large egg *yolk only*
- 2-3 Tablespoons cold water

(filling)
- ½ cup organic (C&H or Domino's) sugar
- 2 large eggs
- 1 large egg yolk
- 3 Tablespoons all-purpose gluten-free flour
- 1 ½ cups full-fat coconut milk
- 1 ½ cups sweetened flaked coconut (Tropical Traditions; to sweeten, toss with a bit of oil and hot water and sprinkle with corn-free powdered sugar)
- 1 teaspoon vanilla extract (homemade)

Coconut Cream Pie

Directions:

(for crust)

Preheat oven to 350°F.

Mix dry ingredients.

Cut shortening into flour blend.

Add egg and enough water to form a ball.

Roll crust out between two sheets of parchment paper. If the dough seems sticky, sprinkle the parchment with gluten-free flour and roll the ball before covering with second sheet and rolling out.

Peel the top parchment and flip into pie pan. Carefully peel parchment off. Flute edges and prick bottom with a fork.

Place crust in freezer for about 10 minutes until well-chilled.

Bake until lightly brown. This should take around 15 minutes.

(for filling)

Whisk ½ cup sugar, eggs, egg yolk, and gluten-free flour in medium bowl.

Bring coconut milk and sweetened coconut to simmer in a saucepan over medium heat.

Gradually add hot coconut mixture to egg mixture, whisking the whole time. Return to the saucepan and cook, stirring constantly, until cream thickens and boils. This should take 3-4 minutes.

Remove from heat.

Mix in vanilla extract. Transfer cream to bowl. Press plastic wrap directly onto surface to prevent skin formation. Chill at least 2 hours, and up to 1 day. Once chilled, place filling in crust.

Before serving, top with coconut whipped cream and some toasted coconut.

Everyday Blueberry Muffins

Everyday Blueberry Muffins

Ingredients

- 2 ¼ cups all-purpose gluten-free flour
- 1 Tablespoon baking powder (homemade)
- ½ teaspoon salt (pink Himalayan)
- ½ teaspoon guar gum (NOW brand)
- ¾ cup organic granulated sugar (Domino's or C&H)
- 6 Tablespoons grapeseed oil
- ½ cup plain full-fat coconut yogurt (homemade)
- 3 large beaten eggs *yolks?*
- 1 teaspoon vanilla extract (homemade)
- 1 ½ cups frozen wild blueberries (that you either picked or sourced carefully!)
- 2 Tablespoons organic granulated sugar (for topping)

Directions:

Preheat oven to 375°F.

In mixing bowl, combine flour, baking powder, salt, guar gum, and ¾ cup of granulated sugar.

Add grapeseed oil, coconut yogurt, eggs, and vanilla extract. Mix just until dry ingredients are wet. Add frozen blueberries last (you don't have to thaw and rinse).

Scoop finished batter into greased muffin tin or paper. Papers can have hidden corn, so choose them carefully. Fill tins or papers about ¾ full. Sprinkle filled muffins with granulated sugar.

Bake 20-23 minutes. Makes at least 18 muffins.

Because of the blueberries' moisture, these keep well for a couple of days. They can be individually wrapped and frozen if desired.

If you don't want your batter to turn blue from the berries, you can alleviate the problem. Thaw the berries, rinse and drain them, and then pat dry before adding to the mix. This will reduce the baking time by a minute or two.

Chickpea "Pecan" Pie

Ingredients:

(crust)

- 1 ¼ cups gluten-free all-purpose flour (homemade)
- 1 Tablespoon C&H organic cane sugar
- ½ teaspoon NOW brand guar gum
- ½ teaspoon salt (pink Himalayan)
- 6 Tablespoons cold Tropical Traditions palm shortening
- 1 large egg
- 2-3 Tablespoons cold water (depending on flour blend

Chickpea "Pecan" Pie

(filling)
- 1 cup packed light brown sugar (or dark muscovado, turbinado, or dark brown sugar)
- ⅔ cup Lyle's golden syrup
- 4 Tablespoons Tropical Traditions coconut oil, plus more for coating pie plate
- 3 large eggs
- 1-1 ¼ cups roasted chickpea nuts (homemade)
- 1 Tablespoon vanilla extract (homemade)
- ¼ teaspoon salt (pink Himalayan)

Directions:

(for crust)

Mix dry ingredients. Cut shortening into flour blend. Add egg and enough water to form a ball.

Roll crust out between two sheets of parchment paper. If the dough seems sticky, sprinkle the parchment with gluten-free flour and roll the ball in it before covering with the second sheet and rolling out.

Peel off the top sheet of parchment paper and flip rolled dough into pie pan, then carefully peel the remaining sheet of parchment off the crust dough and gently settle the crust into the pie dish. Flute edge.

Place in freezer for about ten minutes until well-chilled.

(for filling)

Place the sugar, syrup, and coconut oil in a large saucepan over medium heat and bring to a boil. Boil for 1 minute, stirring constantly, and scraping back in any foam that clings to the sides of the pan. Remove the pan from the heat and set aside to cool until lukewarm, at least 15 minutes. If the syrup is too hot when you add the eggs, they will scramble, and you don't want that.

Beat the eggs in a small bowl until well-scrambled, then beat the eggs into the cooled syrup. Add the chickpeas, vanilla, and salt, and stir to combine. Pour into the chilled pie shell.

Bake until the filling is set but still slightly wobbly at the center, about 40-50 minutes. Cool the pie completely on a wire rack. Serve at room temperature, with whipped coconut cream or vanilla coconut ice cream if desired.

Cinnamon Rolls

Cinnamon Rolls

Ingredients:

(jelly roll)

- 4 eggs
- ¾ cup sugar (organic cane Domino's)
- ¼ cup water (Crystal Geyser)
- 1 teaspoon vanilla (homemade)
- 1 cup gluten-free all-purpose flour
- 1 teaspoon baking powder (homemade)
- ¼ teaspoon salt (pink Himalayan)

(filling)

- 1 cup homemade sweetened condensed coconut milk
- ¼ cup crushed roasted chickpeas (homemade)
- ¼ cup flaked coconut (Tropical Traditions)
- ¼ cup diced figs (soaked in hot water and vanilla)
- 1 teaspoon ground ginger
- 1 teaspoon allspice
- ¼ teaspoon cloves

Directions:

(for cake)

Preheat oven to 375°F and line a 10"x15" jelly roll pan with parchment paper.

Beat eggs until they are yellow and fluffy. Add sugar, then water and vanilla. Add the rest of the dry ingredients and mix well. Pour onto a parchment lined 10"x15" pan. Bake until the cake springs back, approximately 10-12 minutes.

While still hot, roll cake up (short side) and allow to cool for 10-15 minutes while rolled. Make your filling. Gently unroll cake and spread with filling. Roll back up. Allow to cool or place in fridge. Sift corn-free powdered sugar across the jelly roll before serving.

(for filling)

Combine all ingredients and spread on cake. Roll up and chill.

Coconut Caramel Thumbprint Cookies

Ingredients:

- ½ cup palm shortening (Tropical Traditions)
- ¼ cup coconut oil (Tropical Traditions)
- ⅔ cup organic cane sugar (or coconut sugar)
- 1 large egg *yolk only.*
- 1 teaspoon vanilla (homemade)
- 2 ½ cups gluten-free all-purpose flour
- ½ teaspoon guar gum (NOW brand)
- 1 teaspoon baking powder(homemade)
- ¼ teaspoon baking soda
- dash of salt
- coconut flakes (Tropical Traditions)
- egg white + 1 teaspoon water

Directions:

Cream together the palm shortening, coconut oil, and sugar until light and fluffy. Beat in the egg and vanilla.

In a separate bowl, thoroughly combine the flour, guar gum, salt, baking powder, and baking soda.

Add the dry ingredients to the wet ones, beating with the mixer on low until all the dry ingredients are moistened.

Cover and chill the dough 1 hour.

Preheat the oven to 350°F.

Line cookie sheets with parchment paper or a silicone mat.

Roll a portion of dough into balls the size of large walnuts.

Mix the egg white with the water in a separate bowl.

Dip cookie dough ball into the egg white and then in another bowl filled with coconut shreds.

Roll the dipped-in-egg-white cookie dough ball until well-covered with coconut.

Place them about 2 inches apart on the cookie sheets. Press your thumb into the center of each ball to make a deep impression.

Bake for 8-10 minutes or until the edges of the cookies begin to brown slightly.

If your cookies have spread or your thumbprint has filled in some, take the handle end of a wooden spoon or use your finger to gently press the center back in. Be gentle, or the cookies will crack.

Cool on the cookie sheet for 5 minutes, then transfer to a wire rack to cool completely.

Once cookies are cool, fill your thumbprints with warm coconut caramel or jam.

Abby's Ultimate Dairy-Free Corn-Free Nut-Free Eggnog

Abby's Ultimate Dairy-Free Corn-Free Nut-Free Eggnog

Ingredients:

- 2 cans full-fat coconut milk
- 1 cup sweetened condensed coconut milk (or ¾ cup sugar plus ¼ cup additional coconut milk)
- ½ cup rice milk (or other non-dairy homemade milk of your choice)
- 4 egg yolks (fresh eggs are best)
- ½ teaspoon mace (or to taste)
- ½ teaspoon nutmeg (or to taste)
- 1 teaspoon vanilla extract (more or less to taste)
- dash of salt

Directions:

Put all of the ingredients into your blender. Blend well.

Pour blended mixture into saucepan and warm on medium heat until it thickens slightly. **DO NOT BOIL!** You will ruin the eggs. If you get scrambled eggs, you can salvage the mixture by straining out the scrambled eggs!

You want it to heat for safety reasons and to lend a thickness and richness to your finished product.

Allow to cool down some then pour into container and refrigerate overnight or until completely chilled.

If your eggnog gets too thick when chilled, pour the cold eggnog into your blender, and blend in ½ cup rice milk at a time until the consistency appeals to you.

Warm Spiced Pear Sauce & Sugared Pie Crust Dippers

Ingredients:

(sticks)
- 1 ¼ cups gluten-free flour blend
- ⅔ cup cold palm shortening plus 1 generous Tablespoon solid coconut oil (Tropical Traditions)
- ¼ – ½ teaspoon salt
- ⅔ Tablespoon ice cold water
- granulated or coarse sugar for sprinkling

(sauce)
- 3-4 organic pears
- ⅓ cup water
- ginger syrup (or ginger powder and additional organic sugar)
- ¼ cup sugar (you can omit this if your pears are very sweet)
- ½ teaspoon allspice
- shake of nutmeg
- shake of mace

Directions:

(starting the dippers)

Cut the palm shortening and coconut oil into flour and salt. I do this with two butter knives or pastry cutter or cut in food processor.

Once your fat is well-distributed, add cold water, 1 Tablespoon at a time, until it comes together. Too much water will make a tough crust, so be sparing. When it sticks together when you form it into a ball, cover and chill for an hour.

While you are waiting for your crust to chill, you can make your pear sauce.

(starting the pear sauce)

In a saucepan add all the ingredients. Add as much ginger syrup as you would like, this will depend on the syrup you have; ours is homemade and the level of intensity varies. You can always add more later on. Cover and simmer on medium-low heat until pears are tender.

This took almost an hour; keep an eye on it, you don't want to let it burn. If you notice you have very juicy pears go ahead and simmer uncovered to evaporate some of the liquids.

Turn it off and stick it on a back burner while you work on your dippers.

(rolling the dippers)

I have found rolling gluten-free crust between sheets of parchment paper works best for me.

You will want to roll your dough to the same thickness you would for a pie crust.
Once rolled, remove the top piece of parchment. Sprinkle the pie crust with water and sugar. Cut dough into long slices and transfer to cookie sheet.

Bake at 350°F for 12-17 minutes. Bake time will vary on how thick you rolled your dough. You want them to be crisp and lightly browned.

One cooked, remove from oven and set aside to cool. If not using immediately, store cooled dippers in airtight container.

(finishing the pear sauce)

If your pears look like they are too juicy, go ahead and drain off some pear juice. Save the juice for another project if desired.

Put chunks of pear into blender and blend until smooth. At this point, it's ready to eat.

You don't have to use the dippers with just pear sauce. They'd be delicious with anything that's dippable, be it fruit sauce or caramel.

Nickerdoodles (Nofu Snickerdoodles)

Nickerdoodles (Nofu Snickerdoodles)

While Abby does fine with eggs most of the time, I do worry that if she lost eggs we would be lost. I had nofu in the fridge and decided to substitute nofu for egg. It worked perfectly! The coconut oil works well in snickerdoodles, it provides that nice, almost chewy texture we all love.

Ingredients:

(dough)
- ¾ cup C&H organic cane sugar
- ½ cup Tropical Traditions coconut oil
- 1 ¼ cups + 2 Tablespoons all-purpose gluten-free flour
- ¼ cup nofu
- 1 teaspoon cream of tartar
- ½ teaspoon baking soda
- ½ teaspoon vanilla extract (homemade)
- ⅛ teaspoon salt (pink Himalayan)

(sugar & spice mixture)
- 3 Tablespoons C&H organic sugar
- 1 teaspoon ground ginger
- ½ teaspoon cloves
- cinnamon to replace ginger and cloves (*optional*)

Directions:

Heat oven to 400°F.

Combine ¾ cup sugar, coconut oil, and chickpea nofu in blender. Blend until creamy. Place nofu mixture into bowl. Add all remaining cookie ingredients. Beat at low speed until well-mixed.

Combine all sugar/spice ingredients in separate small bowl; mix well.

Shape dough into 1-inch balls; roll in sugar/spice mixture. Place a couple inches apart on ungreased cookie sheet. Bake 8-10 minutes or until edges are browned.

(Note): You may need more or less flour depending on your flour blend. The dough should be a drier dough and should take a bit of work to make each ball smooth.

Beanie Blondies

Beanie Blondies

Ingredients:

- 2 cups gluten-free flour
- 1 cup white bean purée
- 1 teaspoon baking powder (homemade)
- ¾ teaspoon salt
- ¼ teaspoon baking soda
- ¾ cup coconut oil, softened or melted (Tropical Traditions)
- 2 cups packed organic light brown sugar (I make our own now with Plantation organic blackstrap molasses and C&H organic cane sugar)

Directions:

Preheat oven to 350°F. Flour and grease an 8"x10" or 9"x13" pan.

Sift flour into a bowl. Mix flour, baking powder, salt, and baking soda. Set aside.

In separate mixing bowl, combine coconut oil and sugar. Add eggs and vanilla and mix well. Add puréed beans. Add flour slowly as you blend. Batter will be very thick.

Spread batter into pan and bake for 25-35 minutes. Brownies made in a 9"x13" pan will cook more quickly. Cooked brownies may be somewhat soft in center; this is fine.

Serve topped with ice cream, maple topping, and shredded coconut.

Coconut Cake

Coconut Cake

Ingredients:

(cake)

- 1 ½ cups white rice flour
- ⅔ cup potato starch
- ⅓ cup tapioca starch
- ½ teaspoon salt (pink Himalayan)
- 1 Tablespoon baking powder (homemade)
- 1 teaspoon NOW brand guar gum
- 4 eggs
- 2 cups white sugar (organic Domino's or C&H)
- 1 cup coconut milk
- 1 cup grapeseed oil (Trader Joe's)
- 1 teaspoon vanilla extract (homemade)

(filling)

- ½ cup organic sugar (Organic Domino's or C&H)
- 2 large eggs + 1 large egg yolk
- 3 Tablespoons all-purpose gluten-free flour
- 1 ½ cups full-fat coconut milk
- 1 ½ cups sweetened flaked coconut (sprinkle flakes with mixture of oil, hot water, and powdered sugar)
- 1 teaspoon vanilla extract (homemade)

(frosting)

- 4 cups corn-free powdered sugar
- ¾ cup Tropical Traditions palm shortening
- 1 teaspoon homemade vanilla extract
- 2-4 Tablespoons coconut milk
- ½ teaspoon salt (pink Himalayan)

Directions:

Preheat oven to 350°F.

Grease and flour two 8 inch round pans.

Stir together the dry ingredients. In another bowl, beat the eggs and the sugar together until creamy and then add the rest of the wet ingredients. Add the dry ingredients and mix together.

Pour the batter into the greased cake pans.

Bake in the center of the oven for 19-21 minutes, until the cake is very lightly browned and a toothpick inserted in the center comes out clean. Cool completely before frosting.

Jellied Cranberries

Ingredients:

- 2 cups water
- 1 12-oz package of fresh organic cranberries
- 2 ½ cups organic cane sugar (more or less to taste)
- 3 teaspoons fresh organic lemon juice

Directions:

In a medium saucepan, bring the water to a boil. Add the cranberries and boil over moderately high heat, stirring occasionally, for no more than 5-10 minutes. If you boil it for longer than that, you will damage the natural pectins.

Press cooked cranberries through medium mesh strainer or sieve. You want a slightly larger mesh than usual; a fine mesh will just clog up and not let the smooth juice and pulp through. Discard skins left in strainer or sieve.

Return the purée to the pan and add sugar and lemon juice then cook over low heat, stirring frequently, for 3 minutes.

Take it off the heat as soon as the sugar is dissolved. Immediately pour into container to gel and put in the fridge to chill.

Fast Cookie

Ingredients:
- 1 egg
- ⅓ cup grapeseed oil
- 1 teaspoon vanilla (homemade)
- ⅓ cup organic C&H or organic Domino's sugar
- 1 ½ cups gluten-free flour
- 1 teaspoon baking powder
- 1 dash salt (pink Himalayan)

Directions:

Preheat oven to 400°F.

Beat egg with fork and mix in remaining ingredients. Roll out between two sheets of parchment paper. Sprinkle the bottom sheet with a bit of sugar before rolling.

Cut and transfer cookies to greased cookie sheet. Bake for 7-9 minutes until just starting to brown around the edge.

Frost with your favorite icing.

Sweet Potato Pie

Ingredients:

(crust)
- 1 ¼ cups all-purpose gluten-free flour blend
- ¼ teaspoon salt (I use pink Himalayan that we grind)
- ⅔ cup Tropical Traditions palm shortening
- 2-3 Tablespoons of cold water
- 1 egg
- 1 teaspoon organic sugar

Sweet Potato Pie

(filling)
* 3 large cooked and puréed organic sweet potatoes
* ½ cup light brown sugar (homemade)
* ½ cup C&H organic granulated sugar
* ½ cup sweetened condensed coconut milk or evaporated coconut milk
* 3 eggs
* 2 teaspoons ground ginger
* 2 teaspoons allspice
* 1 teaspoon mace
* ½ teaspoon nutmeg
* ¼ teaspoon cloves
* ½ teaspoon salt

Directions:

(for crust)

In a large bowl sift together flour and salt. Cut in shortening or margarine with a pastry blender until the mixture resembles pea-sized meal. Add egg and then add 1 Tablespoon of water at a time until the dough will come together into a ball.

Turn the dough out onto a piece of parchment paper. Knead 2 or 3 times and form into a ball, dusting with a little flour as needed if the dough is too sticky.

At this point the dough can be wrapped in plastic and chilled in fridge for an hour before rolling, if desired.

Place another piece of parchment paper on top of dough. Flatten dough with palm of hand, and then roll with a rolling pin into a 12 inch circle, or about an inch past the edges of your pie plate. Remove top parchment paper and carefully flip dough side into pie pan. Carefully peel parchment paper and shape to pie pan (don't worry if it tears, just repair it with extra dough). Flute crust.

Preheat oven to 375°F.

(for filling)

Combine filling ingredients and blend very thoroughly. Pour into the crust you just made and bake for 50-55 minutes. Check after about 30 minutes, if the crust is browning too fast cover with crust cover or tin foil. The center should be close to set. Refrigerate overnight and serve with coconut whipped cream.

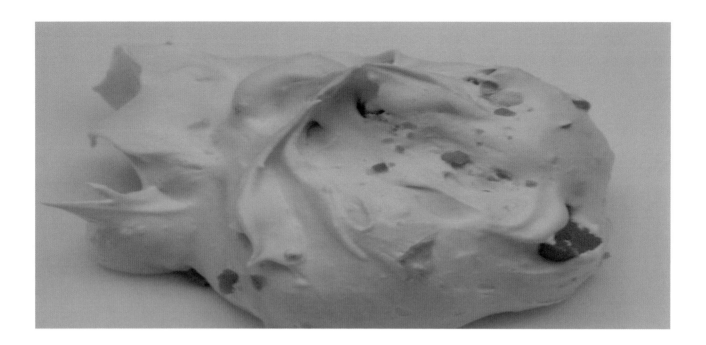

Divinity

Ingredients:

- 2 ½ cups organic C&H or Domino's cane sugar
- ½ cup Lyle's golden cane syrup
- ½ cup water
- 2 egg whites
- 1 teaspoon vanilla extract (homemade)
- pinch of salt (we grind our own pink Himalayan)
- 2 cups chopped roasted chickpeas

Directions:

In large saucepan over medium heat, combine sugar, cane syrup, and water and bring to a boil. Allow to boil undisturbed until the mixture reaches the hard-ball stage, 260°F on a candy thermometer. At this point, remove from heat.

In a standing electric or hand mixer, whip the egg whites and salt until stiff peaks form. Pouring very slowly, add sugar syrup in a thin, steady stream, and continue beating on high speed until the candy begins to lose its shine. This can take 10-15 minutes. Stop occasionally to scrape down sides of bowl.

When beaters are lifted from candy mixture, it should fall in a smooth thick ribbon that mounds on itself.

Fold in vanilla and chickpeas then drop Tablespoon-sized amounts onto waxed paper. Cool completely before serving; candies will firm as they cool. Store in airtight container at room temperature; storing in refrigerator or freezer will cause them to become a sticky mess as they come back to room temperature.

Forbidden Rice Pudding

Ingredients:

- ¼ cup forbidden rice (soaked overnight, then rinsed and drained)
- ¼ cup red rice (soaked overnight, then rinsed and drained)
- ¼ cup coconut oil (Tropical Traditions)
- 4 cups full-fat coconut milk (divided)
- 4 beaten eggs
- ⅔ cup organic sugar (C&H or Domino's)
- 1 Tablespoon vanilla extract (homemade)
- ½ teaspoon salt
- ground mace, nutmeg, or allspice (to taste)

Directions:

In a 4-quart heavy saucepan, combine the rice and 2 cups of the coconut milk and bring to a full boil. Quickly reduce heat once it comes to a boil, and then cover and cook over very low heat until rice is tender, stirring several times. Do not drain. As an alternative, you could cook the rice and milk in a rice cooker.

When rice is fully cooked (should take around 45 minutes), remove from heat and stir in coconut oil until oil is melted.

In a large bowl, combine 2 remaining cups of coconut milk, eggs, sugar, vanilla, salt, mace, and nutmeg and gradually stir in the cooked rice mixture.

Pour into a well-greased 3-quart baking dish. Bake uncovered at 325°F for 30-45 minutes until set but center still jiggles.

Let stand 10 minutes. Serve with fresh whipped coconut cream.

Nofu Truffles

These truffles replicate the taste and texture of peanut butter buckeyes.

Ingredients:

*   1 cup nofu butter, lightly salted
*   2 Tablespoons coconut oil (Tropical Traditions)
*   1 ½ cups corn-free powdered sugar (or make your own)
*   ½ teaspoon vanilla extract (homemade)
*   coconut flakes and powdered sugar to coat (*optional*)

Directions:

Place coconut oil and nofu butter in microwave safe bowl. Mix together until smooth. If necessary, microwave for 15-25 seconds to soften.

Once well-combined, mix in powdered sugar, ½ cup at a time. The resulting mixture should be quite thick, but not quite thick enough to roll easily.

Place in fridge for 30 minutes to 1 hour to get it hard enough to roll into bite-sized balls.

If desired, roll balls in coconut shreds or powdered sugar.

Carob Cupcake

Ingredients:
(cupcakes)

- 1 ½ cups sugar
- 1⅓ cups gluten-free all-purpose flour
- 1 cup carob powder
- 2 ½ teaspoons baking powder
- 1 teaspoon salt (pink Himalayan)
- 1 teaspoon NOW brand guar gum
- ⅔ cup grapeseed oil
- 4 large eggs
- 1⅓ cups water
- 2 teaspoons vanilla extract (homemade)

(icing)

- corn-free powdered sugar
- carob powder
- 1 teaspoon Lyle's golden syrup
- vanilla extract
- dash of salt
- water

Directions:

(for cupcakes)

Preheat oven to 350°F.

Mix sugar, flour, carob, baking powder, salt, and guar gum in a large bowl. Add oil, eggs, water, and vanilla extract and mix well.

Fill cupcake papers ¾ full and bake for 17-22 minutes. Cool and ice.

(for icing)

Mix together small amounts of listed ingredients. You want the icing to be thick enough that it won't roll off, but thin enough to settle smoothly across the top of your cupcake.

Candied Puffed Rice

Ingredients:

- ⅓ cup coconut oil
- ½ cup palm or coconut sugar (or other natural sugar)
- ¼ cup real maple syrup
- pinch of salt
- 2 ½ cups puffed rice or millet

Directions:

Put coconut oil, sugar, syrup, and salt in a small saucepan.

Heat mixture on medium-high heat, stirring constantly. Bring to a boil and allow it to boil for 2 minutes, taking care not to let it burn.

After boiling for 2 minutes, pour over the puffed rice or puffed millet. Using a large wooden spoon, gently stir the puffed rice until all the pieces are coated.

Spread the coated puffed rice onto a greased cookie sheet. Bake for 15 minutes at 300°F.

Store leftovers in airtight container.

Homemade Sprinkles

Ingredients:

*   2-3 cups corn-free powdered sugar
*   1 raw egg white (fresh, never from a carton)
*   ¼ cup pomegranate juice (fresh or other red color fresh juice like cherry or raspberry)

Directions:

Place sugar in a bowl. Add egg white and pomegranate juice and mix until it has good color and texture. You can add more or less pomegranate juice to get the desired color; ¼ cup will give a lavender color.

If mixture is too runny, add more sugar or tapioca starch.

Pipe out long, thin lines of mixture onto parchment paper, and allow to air dry for a day.

After the lines of icing are dry, break them up into sprinkle-sized pieces with a knife.

You could create shaped sprinkles with different piping tips, or experiment with different natural colorings.

Nofu and Double Potato Irish Potato Candy

Ingredients:

- ¼ cup mashed potato (plain, just boiled and mashed)
- 3 cups corn-free organic powdered sugar (or homemade)
- ½ cup nofu butter
- vanilla (homemade)

Directions:

Put mashed potatoes into a bowl and mash them again with a fork. Add vanilla.

Add ½ cup of powdered sugar and start mixing. It will become almost like water.

Continue adding powdered sugar, ½ cup at a time, until you create sticky dough.

Cover a clean, dry countertop with powdered sugar. Knead dough and roll out on the powdered counter. Add more powdered sugar as necessary to roll it out smooth and keep it from sticking to the counter.

Spread with nofu butter or your choice of filling on the dough, and roll like a cinnamon roll.

Slice and enjoy!

Abby's Perfect Pudding

Ingredients:

* 2 ½ cups homemade rice milk (or coconut milk)
* ¾ cup sugar
* 3 Tablespoons potato starch
* 3 egg yolks
* 1 teaspoon vanilla extract (homemade)
* 1 Tablespoon coconut oil
* pinch of salt

Directions:

Place milk, sugar, potato starch and salt in saucepan. Heat on medium-high heat.

In a separate bowl, beat eggs. When milk comes to a gentle boil, remove saucepan from heat and slowly blend eggs into milk mixture, mixing quickly and well.

Return to heat and cook for one minute. If too thick, add a bit more rice milk. Pour into strainer over a bowl. Stir through strainer to remove any bits of egg. Return the pudding in the bowl to the pot.

Stir in vanilla extract and the coconut oil. Pour into a container for the fridge. To prevent a skin from developing, press a piece of plastic wrap directly against the surface.

Serve chilled.

Carrot Bread

Carrot Bread

Ingredients:
- 1 ¼ cups finely shredded carrot
- 2 eggs
- ¾ cup grapeseed oil
- 1 teaspoon vanilla extract (homemade)
- 1 cup organic C&H cane sugar
- 1 ¾ cups all-purpose gluten-free flour
- 1 teaspoon baking powder (homemade)
- 1 teaspoon ground ginger
- ¼ teaspoon ground cloves
- ¾ teaspoon baking soda
- ½ teaspoon guar gum
- ½ teaspoon salt
- ¼ cup Made in Nature figs

Directions:

Preheat oven to 325°F and grease loaf pan.

Finely dice figs and soak them in hot water. Set aside.

In a large bowl, combine carrot, eggs, oil, vanilla, and sugar.

Add flour, baking powder, ginger, cloves, baking soda, guar gum, and salt to wet ingredients. Mix until just combined.

Drain figs and add figs to batter.

Pour batter into greased loaf pan and bake for approximately 60-65 minutes, or until knife comes out clean.

Abby's Fudge

Ingredients:

- 1 cup granulated organic cane sugar
- 1 cup organic light brown sugar
- ⅔ cup full-fat coconut milk
- 2 Tablespoons Lyle's golden syrup
- ½ teaspoon salt (pink Himalayan)
- 2 Tablespoons coconut oil (Tropical Traditions)
- 1 teaspoon vanilla extract (homemade)

Directions:

Line a loaf pan with foil or parchment paper and then grease the lining with coconut oil. The size of the pan depends on how thick you want your fudge; an 8x8 pan spreads them quite thin.

Combine sugar, milk, golden syrup, and salt in a 2-quart saucepan. Cook over medium-heat, stirring constantly, until sugars are dissolved.

Cook, stirring occasionally, to 234°F on a candy thermometer, or until a small amount of mixture dropped into very cold water forms a soft ball which flattens when removed from water.

Remove from heat and add coconut oil. Cool mixture to 120°F without stirring. This will take around an hour. The bottom of the pan will be lukewarm.

Add vanilla and beat vigorously and continuously until candy is thick and no longer glossy. The mixture will hold its shape when dropped from the spoon.

Spread mixture evenly into oiled pan. Cool until firm, then cut and store in airtight container.

Candied Coconut Macaroons

Candied Coconut Macaroons

Ingredients:
- 2 ½ cups Tropical Traditions flaked coconut
o 2 teaspoons corn-free powdered sugar
o 1 teaspoon grapeseed oil
o 1 teaspoon water
- ⅓ cup all-purpose gluten-free flour
- ¼ teaspoon salt (pink Himalayan)
- ⅔ cup sweetened condensed coconut milk
- 1 teaspoon vanilla extract (homemade)

Directions:

(to sweeten coconut flakes)

Mix powdered sugar into coconut flakes. Sprinkle the grapeseed oil and water over the coconut flakes and mix well. The sweetened flakes should be sticky but not soggy.

(making the cookies)

Preheat oven to 350°F.

Combine all the ingredients in a mixing bowl.

Drop dough by the teaspoonful onto parchment-lined cookie sheet. Be sure that you use parchment and not anything else: they will stick badly to any other liner.

Bake for 12-15 minutes, until lightly browned. Allow to cool completely before transferring for storage.

Store in airtight container, layering with parchment paper to prevent the cookies from sticking together.

Microwave Coconut Caramel

This recipe is so easy, and so incredible. It's great for dipping, or pouring over ice cream.

Ingredients:

*   ½ cup sugar
*   ¼ cup golden cane syrup
*   5-6 drops lemon juice
*   3 Tablespoons coconut cream
*   dash of salt (to taste)

Directions:

Combine the sugar, syrup, and lemon juice in a microwave safe 2-cup measuring cup. Mix well, trying to get all the sugar moist.

Cook in microwave for 3 minutes, uncovered.

Mix the coconut cream and a dash or two of salt into the caramel. It will get firmer as it cools.

Chickpea Nofu and Coconut Cookies

Chickpea Nofu and Coconut Cookies

Ingredients:

*   1 cup chickpea nofu
*   ½ cup coconut oil (solid, Tropical Traditions)
*   2 eggs
*   ¼ cup homemade coconut yogurt
*   1 cup dark brown sugar
*   ½ cup granulated organic C&H sugar
*   1 teaspoon homemade vanilla extract
*   3 ¼ cups gluten-free all-purpose flour
*   2 cups unsweetened coconut flakes
*   ¾ teaspoon salt (pink Himalayan)
*   1 teaspoon baking soda

Directions:

Put the nofu, coconut oil, eggs, coconut yogurt, brown sugar, granulated sugar, and vanilla extract into blender and blend well. You want it smooth. It will be surprisingly liquidy.

In a large mixing bowl, pour in the chickpea nofu mix from the blender. Add gluten-free flour, coconut flakes, salt, and baking soda. Then, cover and refrigerate for at least 1 hour. Refrigeration will firm the dough up.

Preheat oven to 375°F.

On a greased cookie sheet, spoon cookie dough with a bit of space between cookies. They will spread more or less depending on your flour blend, so try baking a single test cookie to see how much space you will need.

Bake for 10-12 minutes until barely brown and just set to touch.

These keep nicely and freeze well. You can even freeze the dough by dropping spoonfuls onto a cookie sheet and freezing them, and then placing the frozen cookie dough balls into a freezer container. Frozen cookies will need to bake longer if you don't thaw them first.

If desired, make a glaze out of Grade B maple syrup, powdered sugar, and vanilla extract, and drizzle on cooled cookies.

Crap-Free Cream Puffs

The only difference between these cream puffs and traditional puffs is that these will not puff up quite as much as the traditional ones. Otherwise, you can use them to create all of your old favorites.

Crap-Free Cream Puffs

Ingredients:

* ⅔ cup organic white rice flour
* ⅓ cup sweet rice flour (also known as glutinous rice flour)
* ½ teaspoon guar gum (NOW brand)
* 1 teaspoon baking powder (homemade)
* 1 cup water
* ½ cup coconut oil (Tropical Traditions)
* 4 large eggs, room temperature
* pinch of salt (pink Himalayan)

Directions:

Preheat oven to 400°F.

Line baking sheet with parchment paper and set aside.

In a mixing bowl, whisk together rice flours, guar gum, salt, and baking powder. Set aside.

In a medium saucepan, bring water and coconut oil to a boil. Once they are boiling, pour in all dry ingredients at once, and stir with a wooden spoon until the dry ingredients are completely incorporated and the mixture resembles Play-Doh. Stir and cook for 1 minute.

Remove from heat and let sit for 5 minutes to cool. Then add eggs, one at a time. Beat dough until egg is completely incorporated before adding the next one. It will curd and look terrible before finally coming together.

Repeat until all 4 eggs have been added.

Mix until the dough is smooth.

Spoon the dough (about ¼ cup per cream puff) onto prepared baking sheet, leaving 2 inches between puffs.

Bake for 30 minutes. Turn off oven, open door, and pierce each cream puff with a sharp knife. This will help any steam trapped inside of them to escape, giving a nice crisp puff.

Leave puffs in the oven, with door slightly ajar, until the oven has cooled completely.

Cut each puff open, and remove the soft insides. Fill with pudding, pastry cream, or savory cold salads.

They are best served the same day they're made, but can be stored (unfilled) in an airtight container. To crisp up unfilled cream puffs again, place in a 400°F oven for 10 minutes.

Printed in Great Britain
by Amazon